KISS

"I Wanna Rock and Roll All Night"

Aileen Weintraub

Enslow Publishers, Inc.
40 Industrial Road
Box 398
Berkeley Heights, NJ 07922
USA

http://www.enslow.com

REBELS OF **ROCK**

To Frank Collins. Always in Our Thoughts.

Special thanks to Michael Payan.
And to Remington, for taking long naps so I could write this book.

Copyright © 2009 by Aileen Weintraub

All rights reserved.

Library of Congress Cataloging-in-Publication Data

Weintraub, Aileen, 1973–
    Kiss: "I wanna rock and roll all night" / Aileen Weintraub.
       p. cm.—(Rebels of rock)
    Summary: "A biography of American rock band KISS"—Provided by publisher.
    Includes bibliographical references (p.   ), discography (p.   ), and index.
    ISBN-13: 978-0-7660-3027-5 (library ed.)
    ISBN-10: 0-7660-3027-X (library ed.)
    1. Kiss (Musical group)—Juvenile literature. 2. Rock musicians—United States—Biography—Juvenile
literature. I. Title.
    ML3930.K48W45 2009
    782.42166092'2—dc22   [B]
                             2007041915

5964

ISBN-13: 978-0-7660-3619-2 (paperback)
ISBN-10: 0-7660-3619-7 (paperback)

Printed in the United States of America

10 9 8 7 6 5 4 3 2 1

To Our Readers: We have done our best to make sure all Internet Addresses in this book were active and appropriate when we went to press. However, the author and the publisher have no control over and assume no liability for the material available on those Internet sites or on other Web sites they may link to. Any comments or suggestions can be sent by e-mail to comments@enslow.com or to the address on the back cover.

Every effort has been made to locate all copyright holders of material used in this book. If any errors or omissions have occurred, corrections will be made in future editions of this book.

♻ Enslow Publishers, Inc., is committed to printing our books on recycled paper. The paper in every book contains 10% to 30% post-consumer waste (PCW). The cover board on the outside of each book contains 100% PCW. Our goal is to do our part to help young people and the environment too!

Photo Credits: Associated Press, pp. 26, 30, 52, 55, 78-79, 85; Lydia Criss/Sealed With a KISS, p. 22; Fin Costello/Redferns, pp. 6, 8, 12, 17, 19, 44, 48; Phil Dent/Redferns, pp. 71, 74; Everett Collection, pp. 61, 91; GAB Archives/Redferns, p. 67; Getty Images, pp. 80, 82, 84, 92; Michael Ochs Archives/Getty Images, pp. 10-11, 58-59; WireImage/Getty Images, pp. 38, 64, 87.

Cover Photo: Fin Costello/Redferns.

CONTENTS

In the 1970s, KISS was one of the first rock bands with an
exciting stage show featuring explosions and lightning flashes.

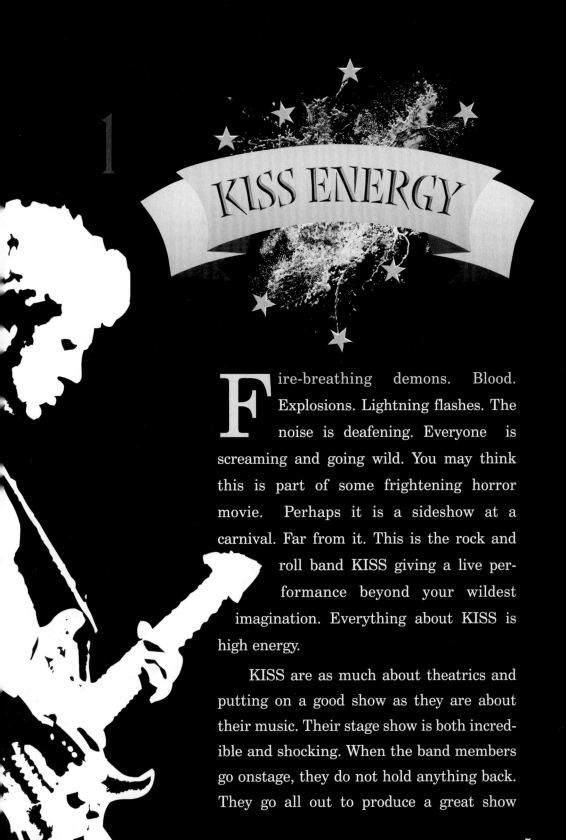

KISS ENERGY

Fire-breathing demons. Blood. Explosions. Lightning flashes. The noise is deafening. Everyone is screaming and going wild. You may think this is part of some frightening horror movie. Perhaps it is a sideshow at a carnival. Far from it. This is the rock and roll band KISS giving a live performance beyond your wildest imagination. Everything about KISS is high energy.

KISS are as much about theatrics and putting on a good show as they are about their music. Their stage show is both incredible and shocking. When the band members go onstage, they do not hold anything back. They go all out to produce a great show

WHEN THE BAND FIRST STARTED, KISS DECIDED THEY NEEDED A GIMMICK—COSTUMES AND AN EXCITING SHOW.

every time. KISS always leaves the audience wanting more. Their fans think this is rock music at its best.

In the Beginning

KISS formed in the 1970s and are still very popular today. Some would even say they are the greatest rock and roll band of all time. Their concerts were, and still are, outrageous and unforgettable.

Back when the band first came together, the members decided they needed a gimmick. They wanted to be different from other bands. They were looking for a way to really grab people's attention. From the very beginning they decided that it was not going to be just about the music for them. The last thing they wanted was to just stand onstage and play their instruments. The band wanted to appeal to their audience visually as well as musically. The plan was to do something that no one had ever done before. They came up with the idea of playing characters onstage. Before each performance, they dressed up in full costume and face paint.

Gene Simmons, the lead singer, was the otherworldly demon with his unusually long snakelike tongue. His outfit looked like armor. He wore black leather, spikes, and chains. Simmons played his role well. He looked like he was about to go into battle with other creatures of the night. "Blood" oozed from his mouth and he hissed like a snake. Part of his act was to stick out his tongue and wiggle it as he screamed song lyrics into the microphone.

Ace Frehley, the lead guitarist, was the space cadet. He claimed that his relatives came from space, leaving him with space energy running through his veins.

Paul Stanley, guitarist and vocalist for the band, was the star child. He thought of himself as a medieval prince brought back to life to bring love to the world.

Peter Criss was the drummer of the band. He was the Cheshire cat perched high up onstage with his drums. His story was that saber-toothed tigers rescued him from a plane crash. Before the tigers disappeared they left him with catlike features.

The "characters" jumped around onstage in leather and spandex. Drumsticks exploded, fireworks lit up the stage, and blowtorches shot out fire. The group sang, growled, and grunted as they ran back and forth in dangerously high platform boots.

The band members wanted to give their audience an escape from everyday life. KISS's music and their theatrics drew fans into a wonderful world of fantasy. Part of the band's act was to get their fans energized during performances. They got the audience dancing and screaming for more. The crowds could never get enough. Band members rallied their audiences by yelling things like, "Do you believe in Rock and Roll? Stand up for what you believe in!"[1] The crowd ate it up. They went wild with excitement. The energy at a KISS show was out of control. KISS knew how much they needed their fans in order to be successful, and this dedication showed.

No matter how outrageous it all seemed, it was never enough. Each performance, the band tried to use more and more stage effects. For awhile, they even had rockets that launched out of their guitars. Gene Simmons explains, "We all have various personalities. On stage we let the fantasy come through. I believe in putting on a show, if people pay to see you they expect you to be larger than life."[2]

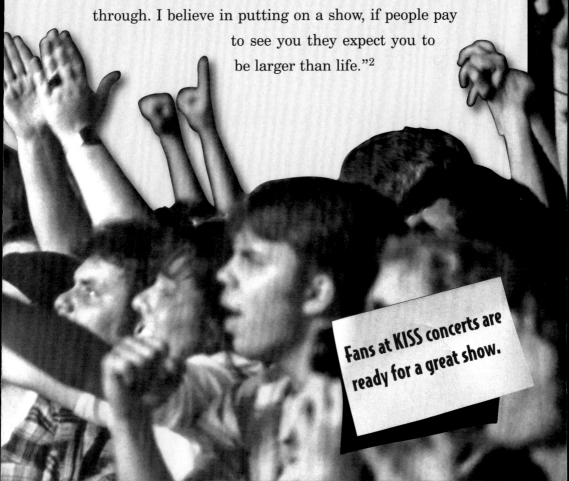

Fans at KISS concerts are ready for a great show.

Early in 1975, Gene Simmons puts on his demon face before a show.

KISS ALIVE

2

With all of these stage effects, the band had a lot to think about. One of the things they had to think about was how they were going to continue to pay for these live performances. Ticket sales helped, but the staging for their concerts cost tens of thousands of dollars per week.

The Next Step

The band's first three albums were *KISS*, *Hotter Than Hell*, and *Dressed to Kill*. The third album eventually went on to reach the Top 40. At the time though, these albums were not giving KISS the fame and fortune they needed to be successful. The band had to come up with some way to boost sales. Radio stations really did not play their songs, so they were not getting any money from that. They had built a huge fan base with their concerts, but they still needed to get their music out to the rest of the world. If not, they would not be able to afford the cost of their live performances. What they needed was a hit album, an album that would break into the Top 10. That was all there was to it. But how were they going to make their next album bigger and better than the last three?

Going Live

KISS were not the only ones having money problems. Their record company, Casablanca Records, was almost bankrupt. Everyone was nervous about the future of the band. They eventually decided that since their live shows were such a hit, they would somehow bring that energy to their next album. That was how they came up with the idea of recording their live concerts for an album. Paul Stanley explained, "Our record sales were pretty soft, but we were building this huge reputation as a live band. We figured that either people didn't like our records or else they didn't capture what we were like live. We felt that we needed to give people a souvenir of the live show."[1] The idea to do a live album not only saved Casablanca from its financial troubles, it launched KISS into superstardom. This move turned out to be the defining moment in KISS history, or, as many call it, *KISStory*.

Making KISStory

Alive! was released on September 10, 1975, as a special two-album set. The band spent four months recording the album, using the best songs from their first three albums. Some of the hit songs on the album included "Deuce," "Strutter," "Black Diamond," the soon-to-be-famous "Rock and Roll All Nite," and "Let Me Go, Rock N' Roll." The album was recorded during different concerts in a number of cities. However, most of the album was recorded in front of 12,000 fans in Detroit, Michigan, at Cobo Hall during a May 16, 1975, concert. "With a sell-out crowd roaring their approval *Alive!* captured the energy of 'The Hottest Band in the Land' (as KISS were rather modestly billing themselves in 1975)."[2] The band was actually presented with an award for breaking an attendance record at Cobo Hall. Until then, only Elvis Presley, once known as the King of Rock and Roll, had sold more tickets to a concert performance there. KISS became so popular in Detroit that, after the 1975 KISS concert, the media nicknamed Detroit "Kisstown."[3]

When the live recording was finally complete, the tapes were brought back to the studio. Some things were added or enhanced for effect, like audience background noise. The album was then edited and mixed to create the final product. Some vocal and drumming sets were also redone. This was to improve the overall sound of the record. Just how much was done in the studio remains a mystery.

This album was different in a lot of other ways, too. The band and the recording company both realized that they had to put a lot of effort into marketing the album for it to be a success. Along with the actual record, the album came with a lot of extras. It had an eight-page booklet filled with concert photos. The album cover itself opened up. On one side there were notes from band members. The other side showed the band's three previous albums. The sleeve of the album showed the characters from the 1940s movie *Casablanca*. This was clearly a tribute to the record company Casablanca. The movie actors are covered in a cloud of fog. The logo reads "The Image is Getting Clearer."[4] The other side of the album sleeve listed all the albums Casablanca Records had ever released.

To the Top

KISS made one other important decision when they released *Alive!* They decided that, as a rock and roll band, they needed

IN OCTOBER 1975, KISS PLAYED AT CADILLAC HIGH SCHOOL'S
HOMECOMING IN CADILLAC, MICHIGAN. GENE SIMMONS HOLDS UP A
STREET SIGN—THE TOWN HAD DECLARED THE MAIN STREET KISS BLVD.
(BOULEVARD) FOR THE DAY.

an anthem. They had to choose one song that really defined
who they were. They chose the song "Rock and Roll All Nite."
The lyrics to the song "confirm[ed] the special bond between
KISS and their rapidly growing audience . . . . What kid in mid-
70s America wasn't ready to rock and roll all night and party
every day. If any one song defines KISS, this most certainly

is it."[5] This song became a sign of the times. It was about partying and having fun. "The storming 'Rock and Roll All Nite' a stomping number. . ., quickly became a fist-clenching, air punching anthem and subsequently became the KISS signature tune. Talking about it years later, Simmons observed it had been deliberately written as such. 'In the middle of the first tour, the record company said, "when we see the kids listening to your songs, it almost comes off like anthems, raising their fists in the air". For some reason, there was a sense of belonging—we, us against them, . . .'"[6] The idea of having an anthem also added to KISS's success as a rock band.

"Rock and Roll All Nite" made it to Billboard's Top 40 and stayed there for fourteen weeks, at one point reaching number 12. The album *Alive!* had even greater success. It was on Cash Box's Top 200 list for 110 weeks. It made number 9 on that chart in its seventeenth week after release. The album was also on Billboard's Top 40 chart for 17 weeks and at one point went all the way to number 9, putting it in the Top 10.

In December 1975, KISS were awarded their first gold record for *Alive!*. After going gold, it went platinum, double platinum, and finally made it to quadruple platinum. When a record goes gold, this means it has sold 500,000 copies. When it goes platinum, this means it has sold one million records. Double platinum means that the record has gone platinum twice, and so on. Not only that, but readers of *Circus* magazine voted *Alive!* the second-best album of 1975. "People had

FROM LEFT TO RIGHT, THE ORIGINAL MEMBERS OF KISS: PAUL STANLEY, ACE FREHLEY, PETER CRISS, AND GENE SIMMONS.

had enough of the hippie, political thing and just wanted to rock out and have a good time," said Simmons.[7] Sales for *Alive!* eventually topped four million albums.

KISS had accomplished just what they set out to do. No longer would they, or Casablanca Records, have to worry about money. They were a big success. *Alive!* captured what KISS really were all about. It captured their energy and their craziness. Paul Stanley summed it up when he said, "Everything had a dreamlike quality to it in 1975 because we were starting to see what we had hoped for become reality. Everyone wanted to be a part of the KISS phenomenon. I've always said that you may not be able to look like KISS, but you can always feel like KISS."[8]

Not only did the album rocket KISS into the spotlight, it actually changed the entire music industry. Until that point, most bands did not release live concert albums. If they did, it was usually to fulfill a contract requirement and not to make a statement. Live albums had never before been so successful. After KISS's success with *Alive!* everything changed. Live records started popping up everywhere, and most rock and roll bands had to have one.[9] As Gene Simmons explained, "We were at the peak of our career when we recorded *Alive!*, and we knew it. *Alive!* was real, and was very much a product of its time—it wasn't just KISS, it was the mid-Seventies."[10]

3

WHO IS KISS?

The members of KISS grew up in different neighborhoods, went to different schools, and had very different childhood experiences. As adults they came together to form one of the greatest bands of all time.

The band started out with the four original members: Gene Simmons, Paul Stanley, Ace Frehley, and Peter Criss. Later, the band was forced to find new members to join with Simmons and Stanley. Frehley and Criss's roles in the band would have to be filled more than once.

Gene Simmons

Gene Simmons's real name is Chaim Witz. He was born on August 25, 1949, in Haifa, Israel. At that time, Israel was a new country and many people who lived there were very poor. Gene's mother, Florence, was a Holocaust survivor and had been in a concentration camp during World War II. Gene's father, Yechiel, was in the Israeli army. To this day, Gene is very close to his mother and respects her opinions. His father left the family when Gene was very young, so Gene hardly remembers him.

PETER CRISS, ACE FREHLEY, PAUL STANLEY, AND GENE SIMMONS IN THE EARLY 1970s.

When Gene was a child, he spent a lot of time by himself. As he got older, this changed, and he began showing off to other kids just to get attention. Gene said, "I had to establish myself as the loud kid, the show-off, the kid who always had to go the farthest, the highest, the fastest."[1] At a very young age, Gene also learned to speak many different languages. He could speak Hebrew, Hungarian, Turkish, and Spanish.

At age eight, Gene and his mother left Israel to live in Flushing, Queens, in New York City. They moved in with family and Gene attended a Jewish private school called a yeshiva. He went to school six days a week and slowly learned to speak English. It was during this time that he changed his name from Chaim Witz to Gene Klein. Klein had been his mother's maiden name. He chose the name Gene because it sounded more American. After going to yeshiva for a year, he and his mother moved to Brooklyn where he attended public school.

As a child, Gene's big interests were television and comic books. He loved to run home after school and watch television. One of the big moments of his childhood was when he watched the Beatles perform live on television's *Ed Sullivan Show* in February 1964. This was the first time Gene really thought about the idea of becoming a rock star. He said, "They came on stage and the entire Beatles phenomenon just hit me like a ton of bricks, all at once, as hard as anything had ever hit me."[2] Gene really admired the Beatles, an English rock band, and he wanted to have the fame that they had. He also really liked

the idea that girls went crazy for the Beatles. He thought that if he was in a band, girls would go crazy for him too!

Gene began to enter dance contests at school. Eventually, he put together his first band with two other students. The band was called Lynx. Being in a band got Gene a lot of attention. He explained, "The seeds of what would later be KISS were all planted during this period: television, the Beatles, superheroes, science fiction, girls."[3] As Gene got older, he began to take music more seriously. He joined a band called the Long Island Sound and played mostly at country clubs.

After high school, Gene left New York City and went to Sullivan Community College in South Fallsburg, New York, where he majored in theology, the study of religion. He took a job as a lifeguard at a hotel and joined a band called Bullfrog Beer. His college years took place during the 1970s. This was a time of political change, protests, and the Vietnam War. Gene managed to stay away from all that.

After getting his two-year associate degree, Gene moved back to New York City and went to Richmond College in Staten Island. He made a deal with his mother that he would finish college. After that he put all his energy into becoming a rock and roll star.

It took a while for Klein to reach superstardom. He had many other jobs while he tried to make it big, including working as an elementary school teacher. When he met Stanley in

the mid-1970s, Klein still had big dreams of becoming a rock and roll legend.

Paul Stanley

Paul Stanley was born in New York City on January, 20, 1952, with the name Stanley Eisen. Paul lived with his sister and parents in a small apartment because they did not have much money. His family was the only Jewish family in the neighborhood. Because he was a different religion, he ended up in a lot of fights with neighborhood kids.

In 1960, Paul and his family moved to Queens, not too far from where Gene and his mother lived. Paul kept to himself, but the neighborhood parents considered him a bad influence because he was always getting into fights. Most parents did not want their kids to play with Paul because he was considered too wild.

Paul never got good grades, but there was something about him that made the teachers like him. One of the subjects he did really well in was art. He was so good at it that his parents sent him to the High School of Music and Art. Even though Paul loved making art, his real dream was to become a rock star. This desire went back to when Paul was about five or six years old. He used to watch a television show called *American Bandstand*. On the show, teenagers danced to popular music. As a kid, Paul had hoped that one day he would be on the show. He knew he was destined for a career in music.

He said, "I started singing with my sister and her girlfriend when I was six. . . . Everybody in my family had a good voice, and we all used to sing together, which is where I learned harmony."[4] Paul got his first toy guitar at age seven.

Even though Paul loved music, his idols were all comic book characters, not musicians. As he grew older, he began listening to rock and roll musicians, such as Dion and Eddie Cochran, and groups such as the Drifters. Growing up, Paul also really enjoyed classical music. "Beethoven is my favorite music. I don't get much chance to listen to it

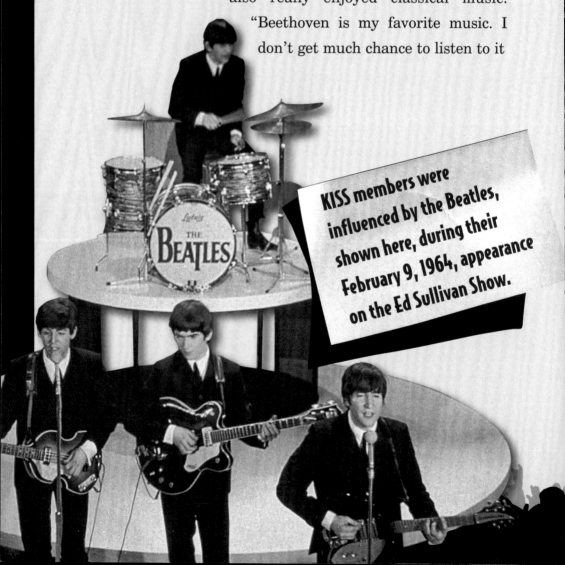

KISS members were influenced by the Beatles, shown here, during their February 9, 1964, appearance on the Ed Sullivan Show.

these days, but the fact that I liked the classics was another thing that set me aside from the rest of the kids."[5]

On February 9, 1964, like Gene Simmons and millions of others, Paul saw the Beatles perform live on the *Ed Sullivan Show*. He was amazed by their performance. In 1965, for his thirteenth birthday, Paul got his first real guitar. Actually, he was not so happy with it. He had been hoping for an electric guitar! He took a few lessons and then began teaching himself. When he was in high school he got a band together with some friends and began to play at parties. He was always the lead singer and rhythm guitarist. One of his bands was called Post War Baby Boom.

When it was time to make a decision about whether or not to go to college, Paul chose to use the money from his college loan to buy a car. He decided that he would rather concentrate on his latest band, Uncle Joe.

Peter Criss

Peter Criss was born in Williamsburg, Brooklyn, on December 20, 1945. His real name was Peter George John Criscuola. Growing up, Peter was one of five siblings living in a very small apartment with his parents. He lived in a rough neighborhood. As he got older he felt that the only way to protect himself was to join a gang. The gang was called the Phantom Lords.

Despite his rough upbringing, at an early age Peter knew he wanted to be a musician. When he was very young, he would play the drums on his mother's pots and pans. The first time he saw Elvis Presley on television's the *Jackie Gleason Show*, Peter was amazed. He even got a little plastic guitar and would stand in front of the mirror singing "Hound Dog," a famous Elvis Presley song. Mostly, Peter listened to jazz musicians such as Benny Goodman and Tommy Dorsey. He said, "I would play along with it and dream of someday being a drummer, a singer, and a songwriter."[6] When he was thirteen, he wrote his first song and even joined a doo-wop group that sang in the subways of New York. Doo-wop is a very specific style of rock and roll in which voices are the musical instruments. The name of that very first band was Stars.

Peter's first set of drums were two paint cans with garbage can covers. Once in high school, Peter saved enough money to buy a real set of drums. He began to practice all the time. This kept him out of trouble and off the streets.

Criss's first brush with fame came late one night when he was at a café in New York City. The band playing, Joey Greco and the In Crowd, needed a replacement drummer for the evening. They asked Criss to sit in. For the first time, Criss got to play in a real professional band in front of a huge audience. He did so well that they asked him to join the band. At that time, Criss was making his money as a butcher. He quit both his job and school to join the band. While playing in this band,

Criss met drumming legend Gene Krupa, who was a very famous American jazz drummer during the 1930s. He was nice enough to give Criss free lessons. After that, Criss began to search for the band that would lead him to fame. He went from band to band and played all the New York City hotspots.

Life before KISS was hard for Criss. One week he would have a lot of money and then the next he would not get paid at all. He even joined one band that toured in a U-Haul truck. The truck had no heat so the band had to cover the windows with blankets to stay warm. Criss also played in a lot of cover bands to make money. That meant he was singing other people's songs. He wanted to do original music. So he joined a band called Brotherhood. It was in this band that he was finally able to write and play some original songs. After that, he joined another band called Chelsea. Criss went through so many bands during his career that he cannot even remember them all.

When the band Chelsea failed, Criss fell into a deep depression. He even traveled to England to see if he could find a decent band to join there. By this time, he was married to his wife Lydia and times were tough. They had run out of money. Criss was forced to join another cover band just to make ends meet. Little did Criss know that things were about to turn around for him.

Legendary jazz drummer Gene Krupa gave Peter Criss free drum lessons.

Ace Frehley

Ace Frehley was born on April 27, 1951, in the Bronx, New York. His real name was Paul Daniel Frehley. As a child, Ace went to parochial school and was very athletic. In the eighth grade, he was even captain of the basketball team. However, music was his true passion. Sometimes he would hurt his fingers during a game and have to stop playing guitar for a while. When he realized that sports were interfering with his guitar playing, he gave up athletics to concentrate on music. Ace feels that playing the guitar from such an early age gave him direction. It kept him off the streets and out of trouble. Instead of hanging out on street corners, he was always inside practicing with his band.

Ace's idols included guitar legends Jimi Hendrix, Eric Clapton, Jimmy Page from the rock group Led Zeppelin, and Pete Townshend from the Who. At age sixteen, Ace went to a Who concert. This was a turning point in his life. The Who was an English rock band and a big inspiration for many. After this concert, Ace decided that, no matter what, he was going to make it as a rock and roll star. He started to take his guitar playing very seriously: "I used to say, 'I'm going to be a rock star. I know I can do it.' I used to look at guys on album covers and tell myself I would be on one someday."[7]

It was around this time that Ace also got his nickname. He was in a band called King Kong. He was always setting the drummer up with girls. Because of this, the drummer used to say, "Wow, you're really an Ace."[8] The name stuck.

Though Ace was his name, he was not an ace at school. He kept getting kicked out of high schools because he just did not care about most of the subjects. After the third high school, he dropped out. Later, he married Jeanette Trerotola, who encouraged him to go back to school to get his high school diploma. Before hitting it big, to make ends meet, Frehley had to work many jobs, including mailman, furniture deliverer, and cab driver.

Though Simmons, Stanley, Frehley, and Criss were the original band members, others often filled in for them. There were times when certain band members did not see eye to eye and decided to leave the band. Other equally talented musicians were always hired to fill the space.

Eric Carr

Eric Carr took Peter Criss's place as drummer for KISS in 1980. He remained the KISS drummer until 1991 when he died from cancer.

Eric was born in Brooklyn, New York, in 1950. His real name was Paul Charles Caravello. He changed his name to Eric Carr when he joined KISS. He thought it sounded better than his real name. Growing up, much like the other band members, Eric was a big Beatles fan. He also admired the rock group Led Zeppelin. In 1964, Eric went to Manhattan High

School of Art and Design where he studied cartooning and photography. During this time, his love for drumming really started to develop. He formed a band called the Cellarmen and played at a lot of weddings and bar mitzvahs.

After high school, Eric took many different jobs to make ends meet. At different times he worked as a refrigerator deliveryman, as a stove repairman, and in a deli. In late 1969, Carr got a big break when he joined a band called Salt & Pepper. He stayed with this band for nine years. In the late 1970s, Carr was mostly drumming for disco bands, but in 1979, he joined a rock band called Flasher. Even though he was playing in different bands, Carr began to wonder if he would ever really make it big as a drummer.

Eric Singer

Eric Singer was the KISS drummer from 1991 to 2001. He was born in Cleveland, Ohio, on May 12, 1958. His real name was Eric Doyle Messinger. He grew up in a musical family and started playing the drums before he was eleven years old. His father was a bandleader and his mother was a singer. By the time Eric was thirteen years old, he was playing drums in his father's band. His father was very hard on him during those years. Eric felt that being in his father's band was a good learning experience, but he also felt that he missed out on a lot of his childhood.[9]

As he got older, Singer began working in a factory making musical instruments. He also took a job in the parts department of a car dealership. By 1982, Singer decided to quit his father's band and try to make it on his own. In 1983, he moved to Los Angeles, California, where he got his first job playing drums in singer Lita Ford's band. After that, his career began to take off. He started to get gigs with many popular bands, including Black Sabbath, Alice Cooper, and Badlands.

In February 1988, Paul Stanley was working on a project separate from KISS. He was putting together a solo band. Singer got the part as drummer. This was a lot of fun for Singer because he had always been a big KISS fan. One of his greatest memories as a teenager was seeing KISS play in concert when they came to Ohio.

Vinnie Vincent

Vinnie Vincent took the place of Ace Frehley as lead guitarist in 1982. Born on August 6, 1952, Vinnie grew up in Bridgeport, Connecticut. His real name was Vincent John Cusano. He grew up in a musical family listening to country western music. His father played the guitar and his mother was a singer.

From an early age, Vinnie loved playing the guitar. He loved it so much that when he was really young, he actually slept with a guitar in his bed. By the time Vinnie was thirteen

years old, he was playing in a band called The Younger Generation. By the time he was seventeen years old, Vinnie was teaching other people how to play the guitar.

In 1977, Vincent moved to Los Angeles to become more involved in the music scene. He began to play guitar and write music with other musicians. He even played as part of a disco tour that traveled across Europe. After this tour, Vincent came back to L.A. and worked on different projects. One of these was as a songwriter for the hit television show *Happy Days*.

Mark St. John

Mark St. John replaced Vinnie Vincent in 1984 and turned out to be the shortest-lived guitar player for the band. He barely lasted eight months. St. John had developed Reiter's sydrome, which made it difficult for him to play guitar.

Mark was born in Hollywood, California, on February 7, 1956. His real name was Mark Norton.[10] Growing up, Mark was more interested in sports than in music. He especially liked basketball. In 1972, he began playing guitar. He took a few guitar lessons but mostly taught himself how to play. He began playing swing, pop, and jazz music. Playing all these different types of music allowed St. John to find his own style of playing. By the time he got the gig with KISS he had been in more than forty different bands. St. John also spent a lot of time teaching others how to play the guitar. He gave individual lessons to students all day long. Besides guitar, St. John also learned to play the violin, the banjo, the ukulele, and the bass guitar.

Bruce Kulick

Bruce Kulick took over as lead guitarist for KISS after Mark St. John. Kulick joined the band in 1984 and played with them for twelve years.

Bruce was born on December 12, 1953, in Brooklyn, New York. Bruce's brother Bob is credited with helping him throughout his music career. Ironically, in 1972, Bob actually had tried out for KISS as the lead guitarist, the part Ace Frehley ended up getting.

As a teenager, Bruce played in quite a few bands, but mostly as the bass player because his brother was always the guitarist. Growing up, some of his musical idols included Jeff Beck, Jimi Hendrix, Eric Clapton, and Jimmy Page. Eventually, Bruce switched from playing bass to playing guitar. Throughout much of the 1970s, Kulick played guitar for disco bands. Then, in 1977, Kulick and his brother both played guitar for the band Meat Loaf. The tour was so big the brothers got to travel the world.[11] After that, Bruce Kulick went on to play for Michael Bolton in a band called Blackjack. He later joined another band called the Good Rats.

Tommy Thayer

Tommy Thayer became the lead guitarist for KISS in 2002. Bruce Kulick had left the band in 1996 when both Ace Frehley and Peter Criss rejoined the band for a reunion tour. After the tour was over, KISS was once again in need of a new guitarist.

Tommy Thayer was born on November 7, 1960, in Portland, Oregon. He began playing guitar in the 1970s. In 1974, he got his first KISS album as a Christmas present. Aside from KISS, other bands he admired during his childhood included Alice Cooper and Deep Purple.

One of the first bands Thayer played guitar for was called Black n' Blue. Though they never hit it big, Black n' Blue was one of the best bands to come out of Portland during the 1980s.[12] They eventually got a record deal with Geffen Records. Gene Simmons acted as producer for Black n' Blue's third album. The band had met KISS in 1985 when they toured together.

After Black n' Blue broke up, Thayer began to work on different musical projects. He even cowrote a few songs for KISS's *Hot in the Shade* album. For awhile, Thayer joined a KISS tribute band called Cold Gin. This meant that all the band members would dress up like KISS and play their songs. Thayer did a great imitation of Ace Frehley. The real KISS liked Cold Gin so much that they were invited to play at Paul Stanley's fortieth birthday party.

KISS played at Georgia Tech on December 1, 1974.

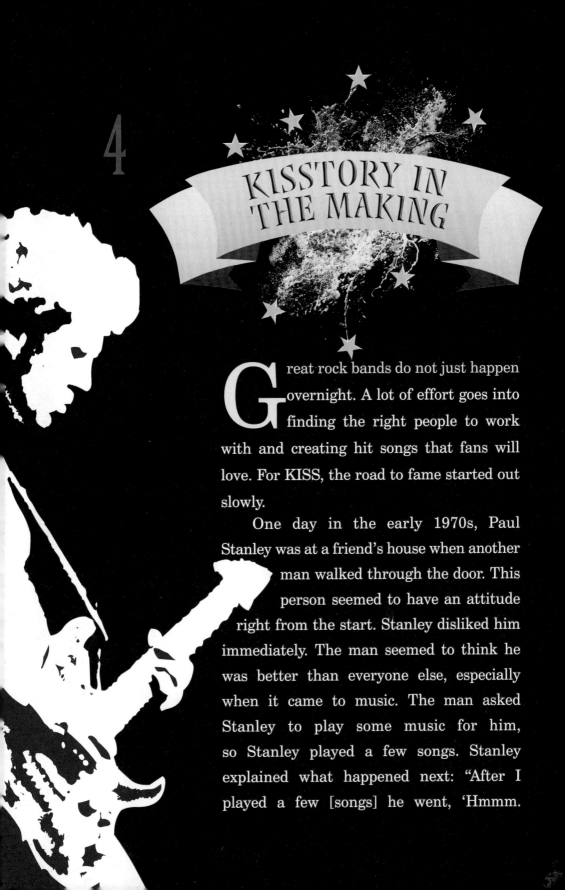

KISSTORY IN THE MAKING

Great rock bands do not just happen overnight. A lot of effort goes into finding the right people to work with and creating hit songs that fans will love. For KISS, the road to fame started out slowly.

One day in the early 1970s, Paul Stanley was at a friend's house when another man walked through the door. This person seemed to have an attitude right from the start. Stanley disliked him immediately. The man seemed to think he was better than everyone else, especially when it came to music. The man asked Stanley to play some music for him, so Stanley played a few songs. Stanley explained what happened next: "After I played a few [songs] he went, 'Hmmm.

Not bad.' He was impressed because now he knew that he wasn't alone in the world . . . .that guy was Gene. And I hated him."[1] As it turns out, Simmons did not really like Stanley either. After that first meeting, it would be a few years before the two would meet up again.

In 1970, Simmons was in a band called Wicked Lester. The band was on the lookout for a new guitarist. A mutual friend and fellow band member said that he had a friend who would be perfect for the band. That person turned out to be Paul Stanley. Even though their very first meeting had not gone so well, Simmons and Stanley became very close friends. After a while, Simmons even began to consider Stanley the brother he never had. They had great respect for each other as musicians. Simmons said of Stanley, "he has always been the kind of person who, though he is very intelligent has to feel passionately about something or he doesn't do it at all. . . . Either of us alone might have made it or might have cracked under the strain of all the disappointment and rejection. The two of us together, though, were unstoppable."[2]

Early on, Simmons and Stanley knew how important it was to write original songs. At that time, little-known bands generally did not write their own music. They usually did cover songs. Right from the start, this set Simmons and Stanley apart from other bands.

Soon, Simmons and Stanley decided that they wanted to make a more original sound, so they broke away from the other band members. They were going to start a new band. The two decided to hitchhike to upstate New York to find a certain guitarist who they had heard about to see if he would be interested in joining a new band. They never did find the guitarist, but the trip turned out to be a very important event for Simmons and Stanley. Simmons said, "The trip was like a rite of passage, a way for Paul and me to bond and to reassert our devotion to creating the best band imaginable."[3]

By this time, Stanley and Simmons were determined to be stars. They began looking at other bands and saw all the things they did not like. They wanted to be different. Other bands just seemed to stand around and play music. They were looking for something more exciting, more shocking, something that would make a big splash in the music world. Now, all they needed was a drummer and a lead guitarist.

In 1972, Peter Criss placed an advertisement in *Rolling Stone* magazine. The now-famous ad said, "Drummer, 11 years experience, willing to do anything."[4] Gene Simmons answered that ad. The very first thing Simmons asked Criss was if he was good-looking. Then Simmons asked Criss if he had long hair. The next day, Criss met Simmons and Stanley at Electric Ladyland Studio in New York. They took one look at Criss and hired him on the spot. He had the right look and that was all that mattered. However, their first jam session did not go as well as hoped. They had different tastes in music. After discussing what was going wrong, they decided to try one more time. This time the sound came together. Simmons and Stanley played the song "Strutter." Criss liked the way it sounded and was able to follow along. Now, with a drummer in place, the search was on for a lead guitarist.

What Is in a Name?

In the meantime, the band decided they needed a new name. They were driving around one day throwing around names for the band. Nothing seemed to stick until Stanley came up with the idea of "KISS." Simmons said, "It made sense . . . and since then people have talked about all the benefits of the name: how it seemed to sum up certain things about glam rock at the time; how it was perfect for international marketing because it was a simple word that people understood all over the world. But we just liked the name and that was that."[5]

Later, there would be a lot of controversy over the name. For a while, rumors spread that KISS really stood for "Knights in Satan's Service." The band felt that religious groups who did not like KISS's music started these rumors. These rumors simply were not true.

Once the band had a new name, Simmons felt it was time to change his name as well. Up until this point, he was still Gene Klein. He was riding the subway one day and out of nowhere came up with the name "Simmons." That was that. He had not put much thought into it at all. To him, "Simmons" just sounded better than "Klein."

Completing the Band

In 1973, after many unsuccessful auditions, KISS still had no lead guitar player. Simmons decided to place an ad in a newspaper called *The Village Voice* to see if he would get a response. Ace Frehley saw the ad. After calling up for an audition, Frehley had a good feeling that this band was going to be something special. Unfortunately, he did not even have enough money to take a cab to the audition. His mother had to drive him and all his equipment to the studio.

Frehley walked into the audition with two different colored sneakers on and just sat down to play. The problem was, someone else was in the middle of auditioning at the time! Simmons yelled at Frehley to wait his turn. When it was time for Frehley to play, he did a great job. Frehley is also the one who is credited with designing the KISS logo. He is the one who came up with the idea of making the two Ss look like lightning bolts.

A Slow Start

In those early years, nothing came easy for KISS. Simmons would actually go knocking on nightclub managers' doors asking for a chance to play at their clubs. Some of these early bookings were midweek shows with no more than three people in the audience—and they were all friends of the band! But at that time, KISS was just happy to be playing anywhere.

From the band's beginning, KISS knew they wanted to be different. Each member wore makeup and created a different persona. Ace Frehley dressed as a space cadet.

The band decided that to help set themselves apart from other bands, they would have to begin really focusing on their look. They decided to start dressing all in black. This is also when they came up with the idea of creating characters for themselves and putting on makeup.

To promote the band, Simmons put together a package with their picture and a one-page biography. He sent these mailers out to everyone in the music industry. At that time most bands did not do such things. KISS began to get noticed. Even from the very beginning, Simmons knew that the way to make it big was through marketing his product.

Times continued to be tough for the band for quite a while. The only place they could afford to practice their music was in a small loft filled with cockroaches. It was filthy and there were not even any windows. Because money was so tight, they also had to keep their day jobs. Simmons worked as a typist for *Glamour* magazine and as a cashier at a local deli.

Making Music

No matter how much marketing a band does, they still have to have great music to be successful. Coming up with good lyrics takes a lot of hard work and dedication. For KISS, sometimes the lyrics would come easy. Other times, it took a lot of brainstorming to come up with songs fans loved. Once the band hit it big, they even hired songwriters to help them come up with lyrics.

The band members wrote what they knew about. They took their life experiences and put it to music. Stanley wrote the song "Strutter" about his fascination with women. The song "Black Diamond" is about New York City. The idea for "Watchin You" came from an Alfred Hitchcock movie called *Rear Window*. Simmons explained, "Our music is very honest, gut-level, straight-ahead stuff."[6]

Some songs came from specific events. For example, Frehley wrote the song "Shock Me" after nearly being electrocuted in Florida. This song was the first time Frehley agreed to sing lead vocals on a song. "Detroit Rock City" is another song that has an interesting story behind it. Paul Stanley explained:

> From the very beginning, the people of Detroit took us in as one of their own. While we were still an opening act in most parts of the country, we were headlining there, and I wanted to write a song about that. Then someone was hit by a car and killed outside one of our concerts in Charlotte, North Carolina. The whole song is really about somebody getting ready to go to a concert to have a great time and ending up dying.[7]

Sometimes one of the band members would simply come up with lyrics while riding a bus or the subway. This was the case with two hit songs, "Deuce" and "Cold Gin." The idea for the hit song "Beth" came about one day when Criss and Simmons were in a limousine. Criss had written the song as a dedication to his wife Lydia. Originally, the name of the song was "Beck." Simmons suggested they change the name to *Beth* because it was easier to sing. After some reworking, the song turned into a ballad. At that time, rock bands did not sing ballads. "Beth" was released as a single with "Detroit Rock City." The band was hoping to have a hit with "Detroit Rock City." It turned out that radio disc jockeys (DJs) were flipping over the record to play "Beth" instead. The band credits this song with helping to rocket them into superstardom. The song also won the People's Choice Award in 1977.

Finding a Manager and Getting Signed

One night, during the summer of 1973, KISS put together a concert at the Diplomat Hotel in New York City. After the show, a man named Bill Aucoin came up to them and asked if they were looking for someone to manage the band. Once a contract was signed, Aucoin sent a KISS demo to Neil Bogart at Casablanca Records. Bogart listened to the demo and he immediately gave the band a record deal without ever having seen them in person. At first, Bogart was not crazy about the

IN 1975, KISS WAS PRESENTED WITH THEIR FIRST GOLD RECORD FOR
THE ALBUM *KISS ALIVE!*

idea of the band wearing so much makeup. KISS quickly
explained their vision and Bogart was satisfied.

In that first year, Casablanca Records invested a quarter
of a million dollars in promoting the band. It was a huge risk
but there was never any real doubt that the band would make
it big. In September 1973, KISS recorded their first album
at Bell Sounds Studio. The album was called *KISS*.
Unfortunately, it did not do very well.

At first, a lot of people in the music industry did not take KISS seriously because of their makeup. Rock and roll bands just did not wear that much makeup and costumes at the time. The photographer who did their first album cover thought they were clowns. The band had to explain to him that they were serious about their look.

Getting Gigs

With a manager to help them, KISS began to get more offers to perform. One memorable gig from these early days happened while KISS was playing a New Year's Eve show at the Academy of Music in New York City. Bill Aucoin had come up with the idea that Simmons should spit fire as part of his performance. Simmons explained a moment that he would never forget:

> By the third song, "Firehouse," the stage was covered by fog. Sirens were going off, flashing lights were blinding people, and the entire place was on its feet, fists pumping in the air. And if they thought they had seen it all, we would give them more. I emerged from the fog in full KISS gear, carrying a sword with the hilt lit on fire and my mouth full of kerosene. . . . A huge ball of fire erupted out of my mouth, and the audience went nuts. . . . It was then that I smelled something burning. I had wanted to look extra cool on our opening night, so I sprayed extra hair spray on my hair so it would really puff out.[8]

Simmons had accidentally set his hair on fire! This incident helped launch KISS into the limelight. Simmons was on the cover of magazines! They were not famous yet, but people were starting to recognize this new band.

KISS continued to do as many shows as they could get. Their first really big show was at the Century Plaza Hotel in California on February 18, 1974. Soft rock was very popular at that time and no one was expecting the show KISS delivered. The audience had been filled with businessmen and record executives. KISS amazed them all with their performance![9]

Another memorable moment in early KISS history was when the band was invited to appear on the *Dick Clark Show*. They performed three songs, including "Firehouse." Simmons will never forget the moment he walked right up to the cameraman while breathing fire. The cameraman was so scared that he jumped off his platform and ran away, leaving his camera pointing up at the ceiling. The band had a lot of fun with these shows, but they never forgot their goal. In the end, it all came down to doing a job. Paul Stanley said, "I remember these early shows so well because there was a great buzz about us, which made it all the more important to fulfill people's expectations. Each time we stepped out on stage. . . . My attitude about every show was that we weren't going to get a second chance, so I was going to seize the moment."[10]

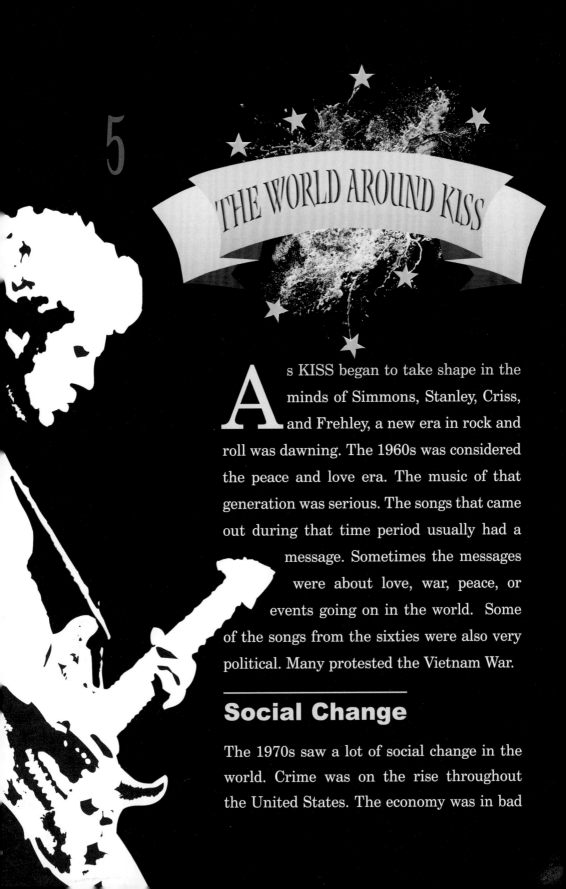

5

THE WORLD AROUND KISS

As KISS began to take shape in the minds of Simmons, Stanley, Criss, and Frehley, a new era in rock and roll was dawning. The 1960s was considered the peace and love era. The music of that generation was serious. The songs that came out during that time period usually had a message. Sometimes the messages were about love, war, peace, or events going on in the world. Some of the songs from the sixties were also very political. Many protested the Vietnam War.

Social Change

The 1970s saw a lot of social change in the world. Crime was on the rise throughout the United States. The economy was in bad

THE 1970s BROUGHT ON A LOT OF SOCIAL CHANGE. DURING AN ANTIWAR PROTEST AT KENT STATE UNIVERSITY IN OHIO, NATIONAL GUARDSMAN SHOT AND KILLED FOUR PROTESTORS.

shape, and the country was falling into a recession. This meant that many people were losing their jobs. The Vietnam War was going strong and was on everybody's mind. One of many important events that took place at the beginning of the 1970s was the Kent State Massacre. Ohio National Guardsmen shot and killed four antiwar protesters during a protest at Kent State University. This just added more fuel to the fire and angered much of the nation. The Vietnam War was losing support from the people in the United States. The war finally ended in 1975, but the wounds were a long time healing. Many people were divided about the war. KISS always stayed away from politics and world events. They were just interested in entertaining their fans and making good music.

The 1970s was also known for other important events. President Nixon resigned from office when he realized that he was facing impeachment. This meant that he could be removed from office and charged with a crime. People continued to fight for civil rights, and racial discrimination of any kind was no longer tolerated. African Americans were winning more public offices, including positions as mayors and congressmen. Women were also beginning to have more say in matters outside the home. They began to insist on going to work, having equal pay, and equal rights. Ideas that seemed out of the ordinary in the 1960s were now accepted as normal in the 1970s.

Entertainment, 70s Style

Along with all the seriousness, there was a lighter side to the 1970s. The decade was also about mood rings and lava lamps, Rubik's Cubes, and pet rocks.[1] The video game unit Atari first hit the market. VCRs and jumbo jets came into popularity. Not only was music going through some major changes, but so was television. TV shows began to talk about topics that had been off-limits in previous years. Television shows like *All in the Family* talked about sex, racism, and religious differences.

The 1970s was also a big decade for blockbuster movies. One such film was *Star Wars*, which became one of the highest-earning films. *Rocky* was another big hit. Movies with musical themes began to gain in popularity. *Grease* and *Saturday Night Fever*, both starring John Travolta, were very successful.

In fashion, bell-bottoms, hip-huggers, platform shoes, and T-shirts were no longer just for hippies, but for everybody.

Changes in the Music World

Sixties rock legends Janis Joplin, Jimi Hendrix, and Jim Morrison died because of their over-the-top lifestyles. They partied a lot and were heavily into drugs. Eventually, this behavior took its toll on these famous musicians.

Another major event happened in the music world. The band that started it all, the Beatles, broke up. This left a dark cloud over the world of rock and roll. It was time for change. The end of the 1960s and the beginning of the 1970s made way for a new era in rock culture. With all of the seriousness of the world around them, people began to look for a way to escape. They began looking to music for entertainment. The music industry was happy to deliver some new, fun, and exciting sounds.

FORMERLY OF THE BEATLES, JOHN LENNON HOLDS A "BED-IN FOR PEACE" WITH HIS WIFE YOKO ONO.

Musicians like Bob Marley made reggae music more mainstream. Bob Dylan was becoming known for a type of music called folk rock. The Eagles were making a mark on the world of country rock. A new type of music, called disco, was becoming very popular in the United States. Disco bands used electronic instruments such as keyboards in their music. Just as all these different types of music were finding their audience, rock music was also beginning to find its roots. There were many different kinds of rock. There was soft rock, hard rock, folk rock, punk rock, glam rock, and even something called shock rock. While all of this was going on in the world around them, KISS began writing music.

Doing Their Own Thing

KISS songs are generally not about serious topics. The band was never involved in politics or any other controversial events. Their music was meant as an escape from everyday life. This was unlike bands that came before them. KISS lyrics were about having fun, not changing the world. Gone were the days of twenty-minute-long ballads and long guitar solos. As Paul Stanley said, "We never sing about the state of the world because we are the world."[2]

The band was determined to move away from the seriousness of the previous decade. They stayed away from all hot topics, such as religion. Gene Simmons has a very interesting reason why the band does not sing about religion. He said,

"On a very innocent level, the worship the fans have for KISS is a religion. There is a kind of KISS nation, and if you're a KISS freak, if you believe in KISS, what you do is *enjoy* yourself. . . .We don't teach you anything. So if it is a religion, it's [one of] fun . . . the religion of having a good time."3

Sex, Drugs, and Rock and Roll

The phrase "Sex, Drugs, and Rock and Roll" became very popular in the sixties. By the 1970s, it had become a way of life for many. Groupies, who were mainly girls who followed famous musicians around, would try to get backstage after concerts. They just wanted to party with the bands. Like most other rock bands, KISS loved the attention.

Drugs were another big part of the over-the-top rock and roll scene. However, that does not mean that just because you are a rock and roll star, you are likely to be doing drugs. Gene Simmons is known for his antidrug stance.4 He claims that not only has he never done any drugs, but he does not drink any alcohol either. He has seen first hand how drugs and alcohol have ruined many careers. He worked hard to create KISS and would not want to take any chances of ruining that. Unfortunately, other KISS band members chose to do drugs. Frehley and Criss were heavily into drugs and alcohol. This eventually affected their careers.

The Glam Rock Scene

Glam rock is defined not only by its music but also by the look of the bands. Glam rock bands were all about glitz, glitter, and glamour. Shiny outfits, lots of leather, platform boots, and layers of makeup were what a glam rock band was all about.[5]

The roots of glam rock began in England. One of the most famous glam rockers was David Bowie. Alice Cooper and the New York Dolls were also important on the American glam rock scene. The topics glam rockers sang about were limited to fame, sex, and getting whatever you wanted. KISS came at the tail end of the glam rock era. They sang about the same things glam rockers did. They also really admired the New York Dolls whose music influenced the later punk rock era. KISS tried to take a lot of what they liked about the New York Dolls and make it their own.

Though KISS may have at first been considered a glam rock band, they evolved into something else. They went beyond the tastes of one generation. They found that mothers, fathers, sons, and daughters were all listening to their music. "When KISS formed, it was the early seventies-post hippy,

The New York Dolls were important to the glam rock scene in the 1970s.

post pop innocence, the cusp of a period that would bring mind boggling growth in the music industry," said British rock music journalist Sylvie Simmons, who wrote the introduction to the book *KISS Modern Icons*.[6]

The Business of KISS

KISS came together because of Simmons's passion for music. However, right from the start, Simmons and the rest of the band had big goals in mind. They were not just musicians. They wanted to make money, lots of money. In order to do this, they treated their band like a business. In this way, they were different from other bands that came before them. Every decision they made was because they were driven by money. Everything they did, from the makeup to the music they wrote, was about selling themselves to the public. "Throughout their career, they milked the market as much as they could by merchandising themselves on a scale probably unsurpassed in rock and roll history."[7] From the onset of their career, they had T-shirts and posters, just like other bands, but they went beyond that. The KISS logo became a force behind the band. The band was known by their logo rather than by the individual members. KISS made sure that everyone knew them by putting their logo on everything they could think of, including pillowcases, cups, toothbrushes, and lunchboxes.

THIS IS A MOVIE POSTER FROM *KISS MEETS THE PHANTOM OF THE PARK*. THE MOVIE WAS ALSO CALLED *KISS IN ATTACK OF THE PHANTOMS*.

Comic Books and Movies

KISS was always on the lookout for new ways to promote themselves. When the band was five years old, they began to look for new projects to keep things fresh. One of these projects was the KISS comic book by Marvel Comics. Simmons and Stanley loved comic books as children, so this project meant a lot to them.

KISS first appeared in two issues of the comic book *Howard the Duck*. The comic book publishers quickly noticed that sales for those two issues were higher than expected. They realized that it was because KISS fans were now buying the comics. It was because of these great sales that they offered KISS a chance to do their own comic book. The comic book came out in 1977 and was a huge success. It became Marvel Comics best-selling comic book to date. Of course, in true KISS style, the band had to make the comic book special. They actually went to the printing press and mixed their own blood into the ink for the first edition print run![8]

Right after the success of the comic book, Hanna-Barbera, the cartoon producers, asked KISS if they would be interested in doing a movie. The movie was called *KISS Meets the Phantom of the Park*. The plot was about a mad scientist who was scaring visitors at an amusement park. The band members helped to solve the mystery and find out who this mad scientist really was. Like everything else KISS did, the movie was a great success.[9]

Shock Value

KISS's plan to be bigger and badder than any other band in the land included shocking their audience. This is why they dressed up the way they did, spit fire, and drooled fake blood. Many times when they were touring with other bands, they would be thrown off the tour. Part of the reason for this was because they always left the stage a huge mess. There would be fake blood everywhere. Sometimes, parts of the stage would be burnt from Simmons's fire-breathing act.

The idea of shocking the audience was just another part of KISS's business plan. Band members never let anyone see them out of their makeup and their costumes. They were trying to create a larger-than-life image that people would be drawn to. Simmons especially was trying to create the persona of a big bad demon. However, things do not always go as planned. One day, Simmons did an interview with a reporter from *Rolling Stone* magazine. Simmons was dressed in full costume and makeup. In the middle of the interview, Simmons's mother came over to his house where the interview was taking place. She brought food she had made for Simmons. She absolutely insisted that Simmons and the reporter stop what they were doing and sit down to eat. His mother kept telling the reporter what a good boy Simmons was. She also kept calling the two of them "hungry boys." After that, Simmons had a hard time pretending he was an evil demon. [10]

In 1976, KISS posed in London, England—the first time the band went international.

KISS: GOING STRONG

With the release of *Alive!*, KISS's career really took off. Five months after that album was released, the band was back in the studio. Their plan was to ride the wave of success. Bob Ezrin was the producer for this new album. He was one of the few people whose opinion really mattered to the band.

Ezrin helped KISS improve their sound and fine-tune all the kinks. With his help, their album *Destroyer* was released in 1976. This was the first KISS album to go platinum. It was also the band's first attempt at writing more serious songs. For example, the timeless ballad "Beth" appears on this album. That song pushed the album to become a hit record. Simmons said, "We wanted to create an experience that went beyond the experiences that other rock bands were creating."[1]

Not everyone thought Ezrin was a genius. While Stanley and Simmons were happy with him, Criss and Frehley did not think he was so great. They did not like Ezrin telling them what to do. Sometimes Frehley would not show up for the recording sessions at all. The band actually had to hire other guitar players to take Frehley's place during parts of the recording.

With the release of *Destroyer* came another big event for KISS. They played to what would end up being their largest American crowd ever at Anaheim Stadium in Anaheim, California, on August 20, 1976. Almost 43,000 people attended the concert.

Going International

In May 1976, KISS went international for the first time. They played at Manchester's Free Trade Hall in England. When they first landed in London, they came off the airplane in full makeup. The fans went wild. They were hooked. KISS now had a worldwide following. Even so, the band quickly began to realize that their popularity was not the same everywhere. For example, they did not do too well in France, but they rocked in the Scandinavian countries.

By 1977, KISS was performing in Japan to sold-out shows. They broke the Beatles' record in Japan for the number of tickets sold. As soon as they got off the plane there, they were greeted with KISSmania. Fans rushed at them. Some even got on top of the band members' cars. The scene was pure KISS madness. The Japanese liked KISS not only for their music but because their makeup looked like Japanese kabuki makeup used in theater performances.

KISS went on to do more performances around the world. In 1983, they performed in front of an audience of 137,000 fans in Rio de Janeiro, Brazil.[2] This was KISS's largest crowd ever.

Platinum and More Platinum

In between tours, KISS was busy working on new material. For awhile, it seemed that everything they touched turned to platinum. Their album *Love Gun*, out in 1977, went platinum before it was even released. The sales were based on advance orders. It became KISS's best-selling album. The next album, *KISS Alive II*, was recorded

KISS APPEARED ON THIS 1977 SPECIAL EDITION OF *CREEM* MAGAZINE.

during three performances in California. This was their fourth album to go platinum.

For a time, KISS was the hottest band around. The media followed them everywhere. Each band member had to have his own security guard for safety reasons. Simmons said, "We topped the Gallop Poll as top rock band three years in a row, from 1977 to 1979. . . .We were so much a part of the cultural landscape, so much a part of what people thought of when they thought about rock and roll, it was hard to imagine being any bigger."[3]

Along with their fame, their stage show also grew. They had a much bigger set now. They added elevator lifts to rise up from below the stage. Later, many other bands would copy this idea. The drums also rose even higher above the stage on a platform. The front of the stage actually disconnected and rose above the first few rows of the audience. Most amazing of all, Simmons was lifted fifty-five feet in the air and flown across the stage. Then he would spit "blood" while standing high up on a platform. The crowds went wild for this!

A Few Bad Years

With all this success, the band decided to try something new. In 1978, they took a short break to release their own solo albums. The albums did not sell as well as expected, but each sold more than one million copies. It was the first time in history that all four members of a band simultaneously released solo albums.

By 1979, KISS was back to work and released *Dynasty*. This album made it to the Top 10. However, it was not considered one of KISS's best. Even so, the song "I Was Made for Lovin' You," written by Stanley, soared to the top of the charts. That song became the biggest KISS single ever.

By 1980, KISS began working on *Unmasked*. Criss was now heavily into drugs and it was affecting his work. The band decided to use a drummer named Anton Fig for the recording. Eventually, the band decided to fire Criss.

A New Drummer

Word quickly got out that KISS was in need of a new drummer. Eric Carr decided to put a portfolio together. This is what musicians use as resumes. It is a collection of a musician's work and promotional materials. He mailed the portfolio in a bright orange envelope so it would get noticed. Bill Aucoin, KISS's manager, called Carr and told him he could come in for an audition. Bill also told Carr that if he wanted to fit the band's image, he would have to shave his mustache!

The audition went well. A few days later, Carr was in the band. Before this big break, Carr said, "I was starving, that's what I was doing. I was in a three piece band and I had just given them my notice because the band was going nowhere. . . .

I was in a pretty desperate situation. I auditioned for KISS Tuesday, the next Monday I was in the band."[4]

Now, KISS had to come up with a new character for Carr. At first, Carr was going to be a hawk. That image did not seem to work for him. In the end, Carr's character became a fox.

His first appearance with the band was at the Palladium in New York City. He was a big hit. It took a while for Carr to get used to the superstar lifestyle. The other band members wanted him to feel more comfortable, so they bought him a Porsche. This way, he would feel like one of the guys. It was a true "welcome to the band" kind of gift.[5]

More Problems for the Band

The next album KISS released was called *The Elder*. This was a concept album. A concept album is based on a theme such as a short story. From the start, Frehley did not like the idea of doing a concept album. He refused to show up for recordings. Instead, he shipped some of his solo guitar recordings to the recording studio. Other guitar players were also hired to play on the album. The album did poorly. KISS was losing their appeal. They had moved away from the type of music they were best known for, and their fans did not seem to like it.

With this in mind, they released *Creatures of the Night*. Frehley does not even appear on this album because he never showed up for recordings. The band had to use five or six

The band hired Vinnie Vincent, shown here, to replace Ace Frehley.

different guitarists to fill in for Frehley. It was the end of the line for him. It was 1982, and Frehley was not coming back.

Creatures of the Night was KISS's heaviest sounding album. Unfortunately, this album was not the hit they had hoped for either. People seemed more interested in the music of people like Michael Jackson and Madonna. The upside was that even though KISS was losing their audience in the United States, they were still a big hit in places like South America.

With Frehley gone, the band hired Vinnie Vincent. At the time, Vincent had a band called Warrior. It was while he was in this band that KISS became interested in Vincent as a guitarist. The two bands had been rehearsing in the same studio. A cowriter for KISS suggested that Vincent talk to Gene Simmons about the opening for guitarist. Vincent got the gig. The band decided his makeup would look like an Egyptian ankh. An ankh is a symbol of life and immortality. Vincent's character was known as the Wizard.

Making Changes

By 1983, KISS had released a total of eighteen albums in the United States. The band began to realize that they needed a new gimmick to get people's attention. They decided to make a bold move. They were going to take off their makeup for the first time. Their first appearance without makeup was on MTV in 1983. They also released their first album without makeup. It was called *Lick It Up*. Taking the makeup off turned out to be a good move. When the album was released, it immediately tripled the sales of *Creatures of the Night*. *Lick It Up* went platinum and stadiums were once again packed with KISS fans.

After the release of this album, the band realized that Vinnie Vincent was not the right guitarist for them. They had too many creative differences. The next guitarist they hired was Mark St. John. He was picked from about one hundred other people to be the newest guitar player for KISS. He made only one record with the band, *Animalize*.

The band was going through one guitarist after another. Would KISS ever be the same again? In 1984, they hired Bruce Kulick. Kulick would get his big break with KISS when he began doing studio work for the band. He played guitar on a couple of different tracks for their recordings. When it became clear that Mark St. John was not going to be able to play anymore, Kulick took over. It just seemed like a good fit to the rest of the band members. The first album that Kulick appears on is *Asylum*. That album went straight to platinum.

Other Interests

During the mid-eighties, Simmons explored other passions. He began to take an interest in television shows. Simmons tried out for the pilot on a show called *Grotus*. The television network ABC liked him so much that they offered him his own show. Now he had a choice to make. He could

IN 1983, KISS PERFORMED WITHOUT THEIR MAKEUP. FROM LEFT TO RIGHT: GENE SIMMONS, VINNIE VINCENT, AND PAUL STANLEY.

either stay with the band, or leave and become a TV star. In the end, he decided to stay with the band.

Besides TV, Simmons also wanted to try his hand at movie acting. He played the part of a villain in a movie called *Runaway*. Simmons was also offered a role in another movie called *Wanted Dead or Alive*. The band did not like that Simmons was spending so much time on movies. Even so, Simmons went on to play roles in a few other movies, including *Never Too Young to Die* and *Red Surf*. During this time, Simmons was living in California while the rest of the band was in New York.

Another project Simmons worked on was setting up his own record label with RCA Records. It was called Simmons Records. Simmons began to produce records for a few bands. When Simmons's contract was up, RCA chose not to renew it. They just felt it was not going to be the great success they had hoped it would be. Simmons Records was dissolved and Simmons got back to work with KISS. It was the late 1980s and the band no longer had a management company. They managed themselves.

A Death in the KISS Family

A few months after the 1990 *Hot in the Shade* tour ended, Eric Carr became very sick. He began spitting up blood. Carr had cancer. He found out that he had a growth on his heart and would need emergency surgery. For a while, Carr seemed to be doing a bit better. Even so, he was still too weak to play the drums. The band brought in Eric Singer to replace him.

In September 1991, Eric Carr went to the MTV Music Video Awards. Two days later, he had a brain hemorrhage. After struggling to recover from that, he had another one. On November 24, 1991, Eric Carr died. This great loss to the world of rock and roll terribly saddened both the band and fans around the world. The last song Eric Carr had worked on was "God Gave Rock and Roll to You II."[6]

The Reunion

The 1990s marked a new era in music. Grunge was in style and KISS just did not fit that genre. The popular bands were Nirvana, Soundgarden, and Pearl Jam. KISS had to think fast to keep their band afloat.

On February 28, 1996, Simmons, Stanley, Criss, and Frehley, made a surprise appearance at the 38th annual Grammy Awards Show. It was the first time in seventeen years that the original KISS band members walked onto the stage in full KISS makeup. The crowd went wild. KISS was back!

Almost immediately, plans began for a reunion tour. But first, there were new rules. This time, Simmons was not offering a partnership with Frehley and Criss. He was offering employment. That meant they got a salary instead of getting an equal split of the revenues. Part of the deal also said there were to be no drugs or alcohol. If either of them broke the rules, they would be thrown off the tour. This reunion was not about friendship, it was about making music.

The first concert took place at the Detroit Tigers Stadium. Tickets sold out in just forty minutes. That was a record for the stadium, which seats about forty thousand. This proved that KISS fans were still going strong.

To prepare for the tour, KISS hired personal trainers to get the band back into shape. This way they would be able to jump around on stage the way they did back in the seventies and eighties. They also promoted the tour by holding a press conference on the USS *Intrepid*.[7] This is a huge aircraft carrier that had been docked in Manhattan. *Spin* magazine helped further promote the tour by printing four different covers for one issue. Each cover had a different band member. It was promoted as a collector's edition set.

The reunion tour quickly made KISS the number-one touring band in the United States.[8] They did 193 shows and toured for two years. In 1997, they even rang in the new year with Dick Clark on his New Year's Eve show.

After the Reunion

In 1998, KISS released their *Psycho Circus* album. For the most part, Frehley and Criss do not appear on this album. Their parts were played by Tommy Thayer and Bruce Kulick, among others. That was the last album KISS recorded in a studio setting.

The original band members did tour together to promote the album. To make the set even more interesting than usual, the band decided to hand out 3-D glasses for the performance. There were special 3-D visual effects during the concert. No other band had ever done this.[9]

On February 28, 1996, the original line-up of KISS appeared at the Grammy Awards.

At one point during the tour, Frehley shot a television in anger. He also started doing drugs again during this tour. He became hard to work with and was always getting the band in trouble. One night, he decided to have a paintball fight in a hotel room. He did so much damage that the

band was banned from ever going back there. They also charged Frehley $10,000 in damages.

In March 2000, KISS kicked off their farewell tour in Phoenix, Arizona. The stage set was bigger and better than anything they had ever done.

It had three huge screens and two

ERIC SINGER REPLACED PETER CRISS DURING THE FAREWELL TOUR IN THE EARLY 2000s.

KISS logos. The show began with a short film about the band. Simmons felt that they were no longer performing as well as they should. It made sense to him that this would be their last tour. Even so, this tour became the number-one tour in the world. Simmons began to reconsider the idea of this being the last tour. The band would stay together and continue to play for their fans.

After Frehley's contract was up for the tour, Tommy Thayer was the obvious choice to fill the part. Not only did he know all the songs, but he had actually helped Frehley relearn all his own parts for the reunion tour. He was also very familiar with the band, because he had been working behind the scenes for KISS since 1995.

Peter Criss left the Farewell Tour before it was over. During the tour, he had added a teardrop to his makeup to symbolize all the problems the band members were having with one another. Eric Singer was Criss's replacement for the rest of the tour. Criss came back for the World Domination tour in 2003. By 2004, his contract was up and Eric Singer once again took his place.

As for creating new music, Simmons feels there is really no reason for it. He said, "We have enough unreleased material to keep fans satisfied for quite some time . . . it would take an earthshaking event to get us back into the studio. In the current market, there's no real place for a new KISS album."[10]

Gene Simmons, Tommy Thayer, and Paul Stanley perform together in 2006 in Las Vegas, Nevada.

KISS – NOW AND FOREVER

Just because KISS is not making new music, it does not mean Simmons is not still hard at work promoting the band. Merchandising has always been a big priority for him. Now the band actually has their own marketing company. To this day, Simmons is still coming up with new KISS ideas.

Unlike other rock bands, KISS has definitely gone beyond just selling posters and calendars. There are KISS blankets, clocks, tiles, night lights, coasters, credit cards, a video game, and even KISS coffins. Gene Simmons also has his own postage stamp. KISS Him and KISS Her Perfume is now on the market. Coffee lovers can visit the KISS coffee shop in Florida. For fans who still cannot get enough of KISS, there is the *KISStory* book. It is a huge eight-pound book, all about KISS.

One of the newer projects the band is working on is KISS Comics Group. The comic is called *KISS 4K*. Their goal is to make this comic the largest comic in history.[1] A KISS cartoon is in the works, and KISS also has a marketing agreement with the Indy Racing League. In the past, KISS has even appeared in commercials, including ones for Pepsi and Honda. KISS is everywhere!

KISS IS A MARKETING MACHINE. THIS COFFEE SHOP IS IN FLORIDA.

The KISS Army

KISS has always said that they would be nothing without their fans. Likewise, KISS fans are very loyal. The KISS Army had its beginnings in Terre Haute, Indiana, in 1975. It all started with two very loyal fans, Bill Starkey and Jay Evans. They were so taken by KISS's music that they insisted it be played on the local radio station. The radio station refused. The two fans kept calling the radio station and sending letters in an effort to get KISS on air. Starkey and Evans began to call themselves the KISS Army.[2] Eventually, the local radio station agreed to play KISS. Listeners began to call the station and ask how they could become members of the KISS Army. At around that time, Starkey and Evans got people together to join the fan club and attend the concert KISS was giving in Indiana. This was the beginning of

Fans at KISS concerts wear face paint of their favorite band member to show support.

the official KISS fan club. More and more members began to join the KISS Army. At its peak in the 1970s, the fan club brought in five thousand dollars a day and had almost 100,000 members!

By the mid-1990s, fans began holding KISS Konventions. These conventions took place at large conference centers around the country. The fans came in full KISS makeup, they bought KISS merchandise, and watched films of KISS in concert. Eventually, KISS themselves began hosting these conventions. The band even sat down with fans and did question and answer sessions. These conventions were a big success. Some really loyal KISS fans even got married at the conventions. The bride and groom would dress up in full KISS makeup before saying "I Do."

The band really enjoyed meeting their fans. More important, they felt they owed it to them. Paul Stanley said, "It wasn't too long ago when we were in the audience and paying. The whole premise of KISS was that when you're paying to see us, we feel we owe you everything."[3]

In the past, the band has posed for photos with local fire departments, police officers, and even senior citizens. This is why their fans are so loyal. Today, fans range from big time corporate executives to six-year-old children. Simmons said, "We wanted . . . to let our fans, the KISS Army, know that they were the only reason we were doing this, that when they came to see us live and heard our call to arms—'You Wanted the

THERE ARE MANY KISS TRIBUTE BANDS. MINI-KISS IS JUST ONE OF THEM!

Best, You Got the Best. The Hottest Band in the World, KISS'—they would know in their hearts we wouldn't let them down."[4] Likewise, the KISS Army has not let the band down. In 1999, the "Greatest Band in the Land" was passed up for induction in the Rock and Roll Hall of Fame in Ohio. It was an outrage! Two fans, Paul Carpenter and Joe Apple, decided to organize a protest march to the Hall of Fame. In 2006, two hundred fans attended the protest rally. The Hall of Fame has yet to reconsider.

Tribute Bands

Another way KISS fans show their loyalty is by copying KISS. There are so many KISS tribute bands, it would be hard to count them. These bands are not just popular in the United States. They are all over the world! Some tribute bands come with a twist. For example, there are female KISS tribute bands. There is also a popular band called Mini KISS made up of little people. Another band, Tiny KISS, also made up of mostly little people, now plays a nightly show in Las Vegas. Some tribute bands have both male and female members. Some wear makeup while others do not. Of course, some tribute bands are also better than others. The real KISS does not mind that all these people are copying them.

The Influence of Rock and Roll

When you think about it, it is amazing how KISS has influenced people around the world. That is because rock and roll is not just about making music. It is a way of life. It influences how people dress, what they think, and sometimes, even the way they speak. Rock stars are often considered gods because people worship and adore them.

Rock and roll has influenced people in both good and bad ways. For example, drugs became much more accepted as part of the rock and roll lifestyle. Many musicians struggled with addiction, including Frehley and Criss. Because of this, today a lot of people better understand the terrible effects of drugs and alcohol. Many people are choosing to stay away from that kind of lifestyle.

With all the different types of music out there, kids now have broader tastes in music. Today, both kids and their parents are more likely to listen to the same music. A lot of new bands are actually copying the sound of earlier rock music. This makes fans curious about what the original stuff sounded like. Some people find they like the old music better. "The complaint about many modern albums is that many only contain one good song and a lot of filler. So kids are turning to classic rock, where the whole album is solid," said Edna Gundersen of *USA Today*, in her article "Kids Are Listening to Their Parents—Their Parents' Music That Is."[5] There is no getting away from it, rock and roll is everywhere. Kids learn about the music from their parents, from watching television, and from listening to modern-day pop artists talk about their rock and roll role models. Some kids have actually formed clubs to talk about rock music and share their tunes. They want to spread the word that this music is out there and it is worth listening to.[6] James Austin, the vice president of a top record company said, "Young listeners are reaching for something else, and they often find it in the past."[7] The Internet has also played a huge role in keeping rock popular. Rock bands have their own Web sites, too.

KISS in the Twenty-First Century

A lot has changed in rock and roll over the years. KISS has done their best to keep up with the times. They do not tour as much as they used to, but they still have a lot going on. The last year of the twentieth century was a big one for KISS. In January 1999, the band performed at the Super Bowl in Florida. They lip-synched the song "Rock and Roll All Nite," and 550 women came out on stage wearing KISS make-up. That same year, the band received their own star on the Hollywood Walk of Fame. By this time, the band had also broken every box office record for albums sold.

Into the twenty-first century, KISS continues to grow strong. In 2002, the band performed at the Winter Olympics in Salt Lake City, Utah. In 2005, KISS did a *Rockin' the Corps Tour* at Camp Pendleton Marine Corp Base in California. They dedicated this concert to troops in Iraq and Afghanistan, performing for more than forty thousand people.

The band also released more albums. In 2005, they released *KISS Rock the Nation Live*. In 2006, they released the DVD *KISSology—Volume 1* (1974–1977). This is the first of many DVDs that have never-before-released footage. Also in

2006, Simmons, Stanley, and Criss were inducted into the Long Island Hall of Fame.

Where Are They Now

Both current and former KISS members are still working. Gene Simmons has his own television show, called *Family Jewels*. This is a reality TV show about Simmons and his family. He has a long-term relationship with model

GENE SIMMONS HAS HIS OWN REALITY SHOW—*FAMILY JEWELS*. FROM LEFT TO RIGHT: NICK SIMMONS (HIS SON), GENE SIMMONS, SOPHIE SIMMONS (HIS DAUGHTER), AND SHANNON TWEED (HIS LONGTIME GIRLFRIEND).

In October 2006, Paul Stanley released a solo album and went on tour the following year.

Shannon Tweed. Together they have two teenage children. Simmons also has his own publishing company, record company, and a magazine called *Gene Simmons Tongue*.[8]

Paul Stanley is involved with fundraising for AboutFace, an organization for people who have facial differences. They contacted him to be a spokesperson after he played the phantom in a production of the Broadway hit *Phantom of the Opera*.[9]

In 2005, Stanley had hip-replacement surgery. That year, he also married for the second time. He and his wife had a baby boy on September 6, 2006. In October of that year, Stanley released a solo album called *Live to Win*.

After leaving KISS, Ace Frehley decided to get back to work on his solo career. In 2004, he moved to Florida to be with his ex-wife. He has made a huge effort to stay away from drugs and alcohol. He also tries to stay away from the media. In 2005, he played a small role in a film called *Remedy*. Frehley has no plans to get back together with KISS.

After leaving the band, Peter Criss went bankrupt. He now lives in New Jersey. He has made the choice to live a quiet life and stay out of the spotlight.

Vinnie Vincent went on to form a band called the Vinnie Vincent Invasion. He has also sued KISS twice for royalties. Both times he lost. After that, KISS made sure that Vincent could not use the KISS name to promote his solo career. He is not even allowed to mention the band in interviews.

Bruce Kulick went on to form a band called Union. Later, he joined a famous band called Grand Funk Railroad. He has also released a few solo albums.

Mark St. John went on to do some more musical projects. He also worked with former band member Peter Criss. He died suddenly of a brain hemorrhage on April 5, 2007, at the age of fifty-one.

Eric Singer still plays the drums for KISS. He has also worked on a solo project called the *Eric Singer Project*.

Tommy Thayer still works on KISS film and video projects. One of these is a TV special called *KISS: Beyond the Makeup*. He continues to tour with KISS as the lead guitarist.

The Future of KISS

KISS has stood the test of time. They have lasted longer than almost all other bands. The musicians are dedicated to their work. There is no stopping them. Plans for the band include more and more merchandising. Simmons is always thinking of ways to keep the KISS name alive. Currently, there are no plans to record new music. That does not mean they will not be on tour again soon. Paul Stanley says, "KISS absolutely will be out on tour again. It's inevitable!"[10] The hottest band in the land lives on.

TIMELINE

Early 1970s—Gene Simmons and Paul Stanley part ways with their band members from Wicked Lester to start their own band.

1972—Simmons answers Peter Criss's advertisement in *Rolling Stone* magazine. Criss joins the group as the drummer.

1973—Ace Frehley joins the band. The band officially changes its name to KISS; Gene Simmons accidentally sets his hair on fire during a New Year's Eve performance at the Academy of Music in New York City.

1974—The bands first album *KISS* is released; the second album, *Hotter Than Hell*, is released.

1975—*Dressed to Kill* is released. On it is the song "Rock and Roll All Nite"; in September, *Alive!* is released; by November, the KISS Army, the band's fan club quickly grows to six figures; in December, KISS receives their first gold record award for *Alive!*.

1977—KISS is given the People's Choice Award for their hit single "Beth"; on February 18, KISS plays Madison Square Garden in New York City for the first time; the band tours Japan and breaks all time attendance records; KISS is voted the number one band in America by Gallup Poll; in June, the KISS Marvel Comic book is published; *Alive II* is released.

1978—The four KISS solo albums are released; on October 28, the movie *KISS Meets the Phantom of the Park* is released.

1979—The single "I Was Made for Lovin' You" sells one million singles and is awarded gold certification.

1980—Peter Criss leaves the group; Eric Carr joins KISS. He makes his debut at New York's Palladium Theater.

1982—Ace Frehley leaves the band and is replaced by Vinnie Vincent.

1983—KISS performs at Maracana Stadium in Brazil; on September 18, KISS appears without their makeup for the first time live on MTV; KISS

releases *Lick It Up*, the first album to be released without their makeup.

1984—Bruce Kulick joins the band as the new lead guitarist.

1991—On November 24, Eric Carr dies of cancer at the age of 41. Eric Singer eventually replaces Carr.

1995—KISS appears at the first official Worldwide KISS Convention in Australia; in March, the eight-pound coffee table book *KISStory* is released; on August 8, KISS performs on *MTV Unplugged*.

1996—Plans are made for a KISS reunion with the four original members; on February 28, the original KISS members make a surprise appearance at the 38th annual Grammy Awards in full KISS makeup; on April 16, KISS announces plans for a Worldwide Reunion Tour during a conference on the aircraft carrier the USS *Intrepid*; on June 28, the first stop of the KISS Alive Worldwide Reunion Tour is at Tiger Stadium in Detroit, Michigan. Forty thousand tickets sell out in forty minutes; in August, *Spin* magazine puts out four different covers, each with a different KISS member.

1997—In June, KISS plays in Stockholm, Sweden, in the Olympic Stadium.

1998—KISS releases the album *Psycho Circus*. It is the first album recorded with the original band members since 1979; on October 31, the Psycho Circus Tour kicks off.

1999— KISS performs at the Super Bowl in Miami, Florida; on August 11, KISS are given their own star on the Hollywood Walk of Fame; on August 13, the band's first feature film, *Detroit Rock City*, is released; on December 31, KISS rings in the millennium in Vancouver, Canada's BC Place Stadium.

2000—On February 14, the KISS Farewell Tour is announced. It kicks off in Phoenix, Arizona.

2001—Peter Criss leaves the band during the KISS Farewell Tour. Eric Singer replaces him; on November 20, the KISS box set is released.

2002—KISS becomes America's #1 Gold Record Champions; on February 24, KISS performs at the XIX Winter Olympics in Salt Lake City;

on April 19, KISS appears on the *Dick Clark American Bandstand 50th Anniversary* show.

2003—On February 28, KISS performs with the Melbourne Symphony Orchestra in Melbourne, Australia, where they record *KISS Symphony Alive IV.*

2004— On May 8, the Rock the Nation Tour kicks off in Australia with Eric Singer as drummer.

2005— On April 1, KISS performs at Camp Pendleton during the Rockin' the Corps concert. The concert is dedicated to US troops in Iraq and Afghanistan; *KISS Rock the Nation Live* DVD is released.

2006— The DVD *KISSology: The Ultimate KISS Collection, Vol. 1: 1974–1977* is released; Simmons, Stanley, and Criss are inducted into the Long Island Hall of Fame.

2007—On March 16, the KISS Alive/35 World Tour kicks off in Melbourne, Australia.

2007— On April 5, Mark St. John dies of a brain hemorrhage at the age of 51; *KISSology Vol. 2: 1978–1991* and *Vol. 3: 1992–2000* are released.

KISS
DISCOGRAPHY

1974	*KISS*		1984	*Animalize*
1974	Hotter Than Hell		1985	*Asylum*
1975	*Dressed to Kill*		1987	*Crazy Nights*
1975	*Alive!*		1989	*Hot in the Shade*
1976	*Destroyer*		1992	*Revenge*
1976	*Rock and Roll Over*		1993	*Alive III*
1977	*Love Gun*		1996	*MTV Unplugged*
1977	*Alive II*		1997	*Carnival of Souls: The Final Sessions*
1978	*Ace Frehley*			
1978	*Gene Simmons*		1998	*Alive III [Import]*
1978	*Paul Stanley*		1998	*Psycho Circus*
1978	*Peter Criss*		2003	*Alive IV 2-28-03: Kiss Symphony*
1979	*Dynasty*			
1980	Unmasked		2003	*Kiss Symphony: Alive IV*
1981	*Music From The Elder*			
1982	*Killers*		2003	*Kiss Symphony: The Single Disc*
1982	*Creatures of the Night*			
1983	*Lick It Up*		2005	*Classic Interviews*

CONCERT TOURS

1973	Club Tour
1973–1974	KISS Tour
1975	Dressed to Kill Tour
1975–1976	Alive! Tour
1976	Destroyer Tour
1976–1977	Rock and Roll Over Tour
1977	Love Gun Tour
1977–1978	Alive II Tour
1979	Dynasty Tour/The Return of Kiss
1980	Unmasked Tour
1982–1983	Creatures of the Night/10th Anniversary Tour
1983–1984	Lick It Up Tour
1984–1985	Animalize Tour
1985–1986	Asylum Tour
1987–1988	Crazy Nights Tour
1990	Hot in the Shade Tour
1992	Revenge Tour
1995	KISS Convention Tour
1996–1997	Alive Worldwide Tour
1998–2000	Psycho Circus Tour
2000–2002	Farewell Tour
2003	World Domination Tour
2004	Rock the Nation Tour
2008	Kiss Alive/35 World Tour

GLOSSARY

addiction—The need to use a habit-forming substance such as drugs, even though it is bad for you.

bankrupt—When someone has lost all their money, cannot pay their bills, or has their property repossessed.

cover band—A band that plays music of other bands.

disc jockey—A radio show host.

discrimination—An opinion or a decision based on someone's race or religion.

genre—A type of art or music that is defined by form or content.

gig—Slang for a show or performance.

gimmick—A trick used to attract business or attention.

hemorrhage—A sudden loss of blood.

hip-huggers—A type of jeans popular in the 1960s and 1970s.

impeachment—Charging a public official with a crime, often resulting in a removal from office.

Kabuki—Traditional Japanese drama performed with singing and dancing.

lip-synch—To pretend to sing by mouthing words rather than actually singing.

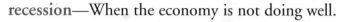

recession—When the economy is not doing well.

reggae—A type of music originated in Jamaica with elements of rock and soul.

Reiter's syndrome—A disorder that causes arthritis.

royalty—Payment based on the amount of work sold.

theatrics—Stage effects to make a performance more interesting.

tribute band—A band that performs a more famous band's works.

101

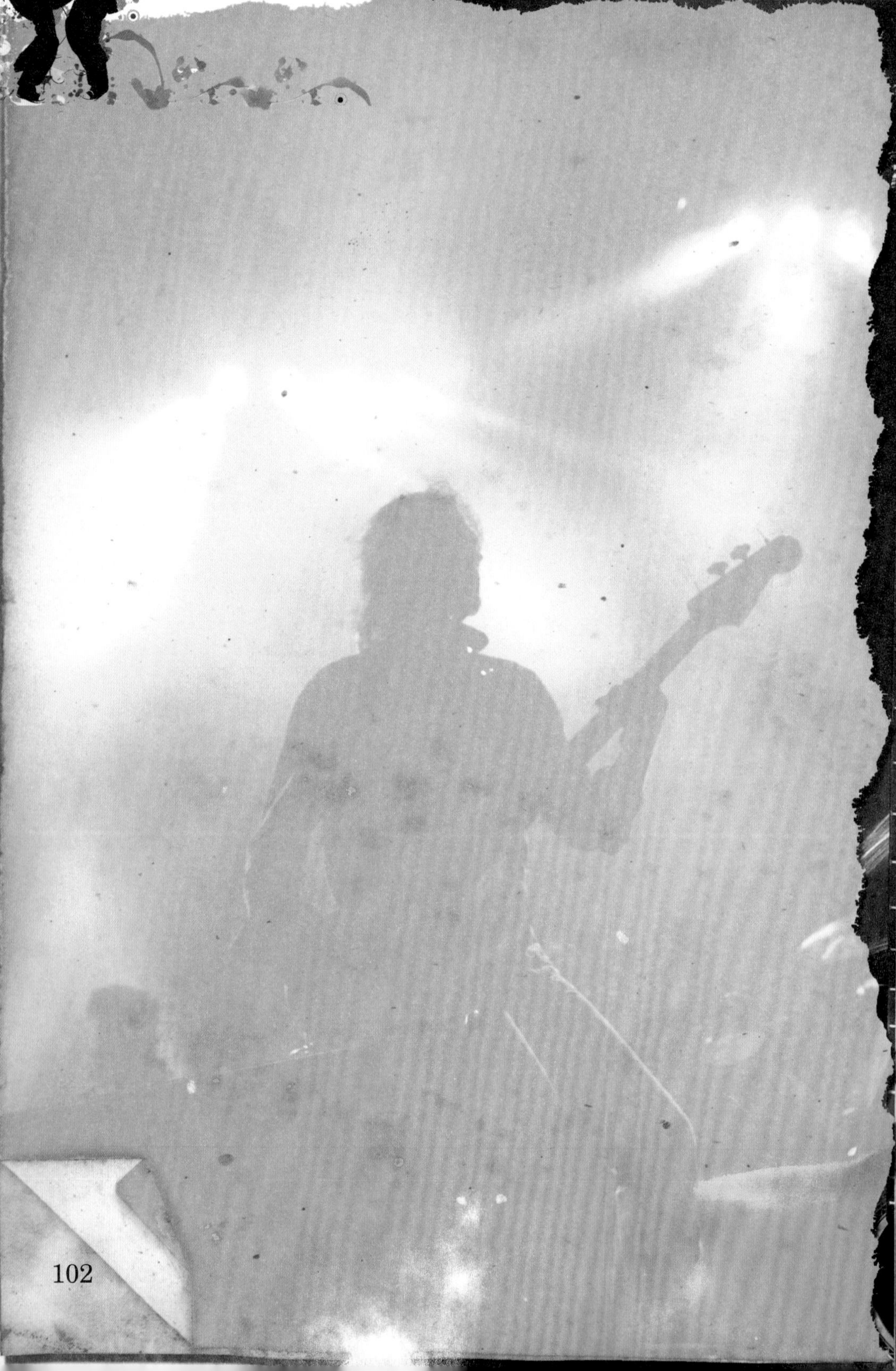

CHAPTER NOTES

Chapter 1: KISS Energy

1. *Konfidential and Xtreme Close-up: KISS*, DVD, Island/Mercury, 2005.

2. Sylvie Simmons, ed., *Virgin Modern Icons: KISS* (London: Virgin Publishing, 1997), p. 33.

Chapter 2: KISS ALIVE

1. Sylvie Simmons, ed., *Virgin Modern Icons: KISS* (London: Virgin Publishing, 1997), p. 69.

2. Paul Elliot, *KISS: Hotter Than Hell—The Stories Behind Every Song* (New York: Thunder Mountain Press, 2002), p. 71.

3. John Tobler and Andrew Doe, *KISS: Live!* (London: Omnibus Press, 1996), p. 10.

4. Dale Sherman, *Black Diamond 2: The Illustrated Collector's Guide to KISS* (London: CG Publishing, 1997), p. 18.

5. Elliot, p. 68.

6. Jeff Kitts, Brad Tolinski, and Harold Steinblatt, *Guitar World Presents KISS* (Milwaukee, Oreg.: Hal Leonard Corp., 1997), p. 9.

7. Ibid., p. 10.

8. Gene Simmons and Paul Stanley, *KISS: The Early Years* (New York: Three Rivers Press, 2002), p. 106.

9. Kitts, et al., p. 10.

10. Ibid.

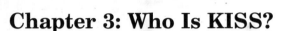
Chapter 3: Who Is KISS?

1. Gene Simmons, *KISS and Make-up* (New York: Crown Publishers, 2001), pp. 17–18.

2. Ibid., p. 37.

3. Ibid., p. 46.

4. David Leaf and Ken Sharp, *KISS Behind the Mask: The Official Authorized Biography* (New York: Warner Books, 2003), p. 13.

5. Ibid., p. 14.

6. Ibid., p. 25.

7. Ibid., p. 38.

8. Ibid.

9. "The Kissfaq Eric Singer Biography," KISS-FAQ, n.d., <http://www.kissfaq.com/members/bio_singer.html> (December 9, 2006).

10. "The Kissfaq Mark St. John Biography," KISSFAQ, n.d., <http://www.kissfaq.com/members/bio_mark.html> (December 9, 2006).

11. *The Official Bruce Kulick Website*, n.d., <http://www.kulick.net/bio.shtml> (December 22, 2006).

12. "The Kissfaq Tommy Thayer Biography," KISSFAQ, n.d., <http://www.kissfaq.com/members/bio_thayer.html> (December 9, 2006).

Chapter 4: KISStory in the Making

1. David Leaf and Ken Sharp, *KISS Behind the*

Mask: The Official Authorized Biography (New York: Warner Books, 2003), p. 16.

2. Gene Simmons, KISS and Make-up (New York: Crown Publishers, 2001), p. 58.

3. Ibid., p. 64.

4. Leaf and Sharp, p. 29.

5. Simmons, p. 69.

6. Leaf and Sharp, p. 217.

7. Jeff Kitts, Brad Tolinski, and Harold Steinblatt, *Guitar World Presents KISS* (Milwaukee, Oreg.: Hal Leonard Corp., 1997), p. 12.

8. Simmons, p. 88.

9. Curt Gooch and Jeff Suhs, *KISS Alive Forever: The Complete Touring History* (New York: Billboard Books, 2002), p. 29.

10. Gene Simmons and Paul Stanley, *KISS: The Early Years* (New York: Three Rivers Press, 2002), p. 10.

Chapter 5: The World Around KISS

1. Charles Gillis, "American History— 1970–1979," *American Cultural History: The Twentieth Century*, Kingwood College Library Web site, September 2006, <http://kclibrary.nhmccd.edu/decade70.html> (June 6, 2007).

2. Sylvie Simmons, ed., *Virgin Modern Icons: KISS* (London: Virgin Publishing, 1997), p. 12.

3. David Leaf and Ken Sharp, *KISS Behind the*

Mask: The Official Authorized Biography (New York: Warner Books, 2003), p. 89.

4. Catherine Donaldson-Evans, "Gene Simmons: The Latest Lifestyle Guru," *FOXNews.com*, September 25, 2002, <http://www.foxnews.com/story/0,2933,58003,00.html> (June 8, 2007).

5. "Glam Rock," *Encyclopaedia Britannica Online*, 2007, <http://www.britannica.com/eb/article-9110274/glam-rock> (June 8, 2007).

6. Simmons, p. 12.

7. Ibid., p. 40.

8. Barbara and David P. Mikkelson, "Blood Money," *Urban Legends Reference Pages*, Snopes.com, May 14, 2007, <http://www.snopes.com/music/artists/kissblood.asp> (June 6, 2007).

9. "KISS Chronology," *KISS Online*, n.d., <http://www.kissonline.net/chron/> (June 6, 2007).

10. Gene Simmons, *KISS and Make-up* (New York: Crown Publishers, 2001), p. 120.

Chapter 6: KISS: Going Strong

1. Gene Simmons, *KISS and Make-up* (New York: Crown Publishers, 2001), p. 114.

2. Curt Gooch and Jeff Suhs, *KISS Alive Forever: The Complete Touring History* (New York: Billboard Books, 2002), p. 127.

3. Simmons, p. 162.

4. "Biography of Eric Carr," *KISSFAQ*, n.d., <http://www.kissfaq.com/members/bio_Carr.html> (December 9, 2006).

5. Simmons, p. 174.

6. "Biography of Eric Carr."

7. "KISS Chronology," *KISS Online*, n.d., <http://www.kissonline.net/chron/> (June 6, 2007).

8. Simmons, p. 245.

9. Gooch and Suhs, p. 245.

10. Simmons, p. 249.

Chapter 7: KISS—Now and Forever

1. Borys Kit, "KISS Seals Comics Deal With Platinum Studios," *The Hollywood Reporter*, January 30, 2007, *KISS Comic Group Web site*, 2007, <http://www.kisscomicsgroup.com/en/news_01.php> (June 6, 2007).

2. Jason Jarman, "A KISS Army of One: The Birth of the Ultimate Rock 'N' Roll Club," *IQ Magazine*, Spring 2005, <http://www.indstate.edu/iq/Geek_Issue/Kiss_Army.htm> (July 19, 2007).

3. Sylvie Simmons, ed., *Virgin Modern Icons: KISS* (London: Virgin Publishing, 1997), p. 59.

4. Gene Simmons, *KISS and Make-up* (New York: Crown Publishers, 2001), p. 258.

5. Edna Gundersen, "Kids Are Listening to Their Parents—Their Parent's Music, That Is," *USA Today*, March 30, 2004, <http://www.USAToday.com/life/music/news/2004-03-29-classic-rock-kids_x.htm> (February 5, 2007).

6. Ibid.

7. Ibid.

8. "Gene Simmons Bio," *GeneSimmons.com*, 2005, <http://www.genesimmons.com/bio.html> (February 2, 2007).

9. D.T. Andrews, "Paul Stanley Honorary Spokesperson for AboutFace International," *KISS Online*, May 23, 2001, <http://www.kissonline.net/news/index.php?mode=archive&id=428> (July 19, 2007).

10. Cameron Adams, "Stanley's Kiss and Tell," *Herald Sun*, February 1, 2007, *KISS Online*, n.d., <http://kissonline.net/news/index.php?mode=fullstory&id=4181> (February 1, 2007).

FURTHER READING

Books

Feinstein, Stephen. *The 1970s from Watergate to Disco.* Berkeley Heights, N.J.: Enslow Publishers, Inc., 2006.

Gilmour, Sarah. *The 70s: Punks, Glam Rockers, and New Romantics.* Milwaukee, Wisc.: Gareth Stevens, 2000.

Gooch, Curt and Jeff Suhs. *KISS Alive Forever: The Complete Touring History.* Watson-Guptill Publications, Incorporated, 2002.

Hayes, Malcolm. *1970s: Turbulent Times.* Milwaukee, Wisc.: Gareth Stevens, 2002.

Schaefer, A.R. *Forming a Band.* Mankato, Minn.: Capstone High-Interest Books, 2004.

Simmons, Gene, Paul Stanley, and Waring Abbott. *KISS: The Early Years.* Three Rivers Press, 2002.

Internet Addresses

The Official Online Home for the KISS ARMY!
<http://www.kissonline.com/>

The KISSFAQ
<http://www.kissfaq.com/>

INDEX